Skye

Books by W.A. Poucher
available from Constable

Scotland
Wales
The Lake District
The Highlands of Scotland
The Alps
The Yorkshire Dales
  and the Peak District
The West Country
Lakeland Fells
The magic of Skye
The Scottish Peaks
The Peak and Pennines
The Lakeland Peaks
The Welsh Peaks

Other books now out of print

The backbone of England
Climbing with a camera
Escape to the hills
A camera in the Cairngorms
Scotland through the lens
Highland holiday
The North Western Highlands
Lakeland scrapbook
Lakeland through the lens
Lakeland holiday
Lakeland journey
Over lakeland fells
Wanderings in Wales
Snowdonia through the lens
Snowdon holiday
Peak panorama
The Surrey hills
The magic of the Dolomites
West country journey
Journey into Ireland

SKYE

W. A. Poucher

Constable London

First published in Great Britain 1985
by Constable and Company Limited
10 Orange Street London WC2H 7EG
Copyright © 1985 by W.A. Poucher
ISBN 0 09 466610 5
Text filmset by Servis Filmsetting Ltd
Printed and bound in Great Britain by
W.S. Cowell Ltd Ipswich

The Photographs

Preface

To me, Skye has always been a magical island. Many writers, both ancient and contemporary, refer to it as Eilean a Cheo, the Isle of Mist, and the subtle colouring of the island, its shifting pageant of rain and mist, sunshine and cloud, is one of its chief charms. Another is the solitude which here, even today, does not have to be searched for: it can be found within a short distance of any habitation. The visitor – be he walker, climber, or photographer – will find his horizons bounded by the hills and the sea; and within the small confines of the island will also find a great variety of terrain and coastline. The west coast scenery, in particular, is some of the grandest and most dramatic in Britain.

My book *The magic of Skye*, first published in 1949 and re-issued by Constable in 1980, has always been popular, and I have had many suggestions that I should add to my books of colour photographs a volume depicting my favourite island. Here is that book. I have set it out as a tour of Skye, starting at the Kyle of Lochalsh on the mainland, through which most visitors come to Skye, then crossing to Kyleakin, and following the main road through Sligachan to Portree, rounding Trotternish in the north and then following Skye's western coast southwards, to Glen Brittle, Strathaird and Elgol. And so back to Kyleakin.

The southern part of the island is, of course, dominated by the Coolins, whose individuality and magnificence place them in a class by themselves. They may not be as high as some mountains on the Scottish mainland, but the secret beauty born of their atmosphere and lighting, their grandeur and loneliness, and the splendid views of sea and Outer Islands from their lofty crests, endear them to mountaineers everywhere, who return again and again to pay them homage.

Owing to my failing eyesight, I asked my son John to help select the pictures for this book, and I offer it to those who know and love Skye in the hope that it will bring back happy memories. To those who may be unfamiliar with it, I hope the book will be a revelation that may entice them to see for themselves nature's masterpiece of the Hebrides.

W.A. Poucher
4, Heathfield
Reigate Heath
Surrey
1985

Kyle of Lochalsh pier

Pearly clouds hover over the island as the old
ferry leaves the slip for Kyleakin. Moored at the
pier behind is the island steamer.

Broadford

Broadford, where the Skye airstrip is situated,
makes a good foreground for a view of the
purple mainland hills.

Near Broadford

(overleaf)

Houses of differing styles are dominated by
Beinn na Caillich in the background. Broadford
is a splendid holiday centre for those who visit
Skye with a car.

The Mallaig ferry

A short diversion from the Kyleakin-to-Portree
road, down the Sleat peninsula, brings one to
Armadale where the Mallaig ferry is berthed.

Loch Ainort

Back on the main Kyleakin–Portree road, the visitor drives round the head of this lovely sea-loch whose rippling waters reflect the azure of the sky.

Lord Macdonald's Forest

(overleaf)

The Highland forests have all long disappeared, but their memory lives on in the name of this group of hills dominating the waters of Loch Ainort. Beinn Dearg Mheadhonach (left) and Beinn Dearg Mor (right) can be seen in this photograph.

Sconser

On the main road from Kyleakin the pretty
village of Sconser nestles on the shores of Loch
Sligachan.

The Storr from Sconser

(overleaf)

The shores of Loch Sligachan yield a first view of The Storr's fantastic buttresses rearing up against the distant skyline.

Glamaig

The burn makes a wonderful foreground for a
picture of the symmetrical cone of this
mountain, which lies within easy reach of
Sligachan. Any walker who is full of energy can
try reaching its mossy summit within an hour –
and will be rewarded by a splendid panorama.

Marsco

(overleaf)

This well placed and magnificently proportioned mountain, seen here tipped with snow and rising in complete isolation from Glen Sligachan, is an easy afternoon climb by way of its northern slopes.

The Sligachan Hotel

Standing near the head of Loch Sligachan, this
hotel occupies one of the most desolate
situations on the island, with the rolling moors
stretching away in all directions, and the Coolins
and Sgurr nan Gillean frowning down on it. It
has been a favourite with climbers for many
years.

Rainbow over the Portree road

(overleaf)

This magical scene appeared before me as I was
driving to Portree one day after a storm. Skye
lies in the path of the warm south-westerly
winds which condense as they are blown against
its cold hillsides, and which produce the great
cloudscapes so characteristic of the Misty Isle.

Portree harbour

Portree is the 'metropolis' of the island, and it is here, in this tranquil and sheltered bay, that the island steamers once berthed. The long ridge of the northern Coolins can be seen in the distance.

The Storr from the Staffin road

(overleaf)

Leaving Portree, the road runs north as we begin our round of Trotternish. This brooding winter scene of icy roads and snowy peaks was taken just before Christmas.

The Storr from Loch Fada

(overleaf pp 46/47)

By contrast with the preceding picture, a bright summer day gave me this perfect 'classic' shot of the Bastions of The Storr frowning down on the little loch.

The Storr from Loch Leathan

(overleaf pp 48/49)

The covering of snow on the upper slopes of this beautiful mountain throws into sharp relief its craggy buttresses and precipitious, shattered cliffs. The Old Man of Storr stands out against the skyline.

Satellites of the Old Man of Storr

This fantastic, craggy terrain is reminiscent,
perhaps, of one's childhood idea of a lunar
landscape.

The bastions of Quiraing

A closer view of this most extraordinary
mountain reveals its riven face and gigantic
terraced precipices, but not its innermost secrets:
they will be unfolded on the following pages.

The Prison

This forbidding outcrop, part of the gaunt and
grotesque Quiraing mass, can, with a little
imagination, be seen as what its name implies.

Quiraing buttresses

(overleaf)

The wind whistles through the great gullies which penetrate the immense buttresses of Quiraing. In this picture the Prison is just visible on the left.

View from the Prison

From this coign of vantage the Needle juts
fiercely against the sky, surrounded by
Quiraing's shattered pinnacles.

Quiraing pinnacle

(overleaf)

This formidable tower of rock is the largest of many such grim guardians of the secret sanctuary of Quiraing.

The Needle

(overleaf p 71)

Looking down on this obelisk, some 120 ft high, is an awesome experience: further below still is the Prison, and beyond that a vast landscape of moors, lochans and snow-capped peaks.

The Table

The southern end of this extraordinary
formation in the hidden heart of the mountain
rises 30 or 40 ft from its encircling grassy
corridor. Its full glory is revealed in the next
picture.

The Table, from above

(overleaf)

This flat stretch of grass, measuring some 50 by
100 paces, would make a superb lawn – or even
a grand putting-green. What a fantastic situation
for a game of golf!

View of the sea

(overleaf pp 76/77)

To the east of the Table, erosion has worn away
the high rock wall, and from here a magnificent
panorama opens up, embracing Staffin Bay (seen
in the photograph) with the sea and the inner
isles beyond.

Strange shapes

(overleaf pp 78/79)

The height, the solitude, the weird dark
pinnacles, the extensive views – this picture,
perhaps, summarizes the secret and lonely joys
of Quiraing.

Looking south to the Prison

I took this study of timeless, weathered rock as
I left the hidden sanctuary of Quiraing.

Staffin Bay

(overleaf)

Near the north-eastern tip of the island, this charming, almost semi-circular bay is a peaceful spot in which to linger. On the far horizon can be seen the mainland mountains.

Sron Vourlinn

(overleaf pp 84/85)

This imposing, flat-topped mountain lies to the north of Quiraing, and is the northernmost point of the Trotternish ridge.

Duntulm

Cutting across the tip of Trotternish, we come
to the isolated little hamlet of Duntulm on the
north-western coast.

86

Duntulm Castle from the east

(overleaf)

The ruins of this noble castle stand on a little promontory, but there is not much to tell us of its former grandeur. The most conspicuous feature is what remains of the ancient keep.

Castle ruins

Sheep graze peacefully on the hummocky grass round the castle ruins, where once walls and ditches protected the inmates.

Duntulm Castle from the west

(overleaf)

The builders of the castle chose their site well: it is unassailable from the sea and safe on its rocky headland. The gable which remains might once have been part of a chapel.

Uig

From this little port on the western coast of
Skye, many visitors take the ferry for the Outer
Isles on the far horizon.

Uig Bay

'Uig' means 'the nook' or 'retired place' – very
appropriate for this remote and peaceful spot.
Walkers and younger visitors may like to know
that it also boasts one of the best youth hostels
on the island.

Dunvegan Castle

For generations this was the home of the
Macleod family: now it has been modernized,
and fascinating relics of its past glory are on
show to the visitor. This photograph is taken
from the head of Loch Dunvegan.

Dunvegan Head

(overleaf)

Frowning over the waters of Loch Pooltiel are
the beetling cliffs of Dunvegan Head. They
contain one most unusual feature – a waterfall
that plummets straight into the sea.

Waterstein Head

The coast in the far west of Skye merits a visit
whatever the weather, and one of its most
spectacular features is Waterstein Head,
dominating the wild scene with its 971 ft of
rock dropping down towards Moonen Bay.

Cliffs
at Waterstein

(overleaf)

In this picture taken on a beautiful summer's day the Atlantic swells peacefully at the foot of the sheer cliffs: it can be a very different scene with stormy weather, when great waves come crashing against the rocks.

Lighthouse at Neist Point

This is the westernmost point of Skye,
photographed from near Waterstein Head. The
huge foghorn in front of the lighthouse looks
like an ancient cannon.

Macleod's Tables

(overleaf)

These twin peaks with their strangely flattened tops and heathery flanks sinking down towards the sea are familiarly known as Macleod's Tables, but are, more correctly, Healaval More to the north and Healaval Beg to the south.

First view of the Coolins

(overleaf pp 112/113)

From Bracadale on Loch Harport we get an early view of the splendid ridge of the Coolins and the mysterious and sombre storm-clouds crowning them.

Glen Brittle House

In remote Glen Brittle, lying to the west of the
Coolins, is this one-time shooting lodge of the
Macleods, which was for many years also a
haven for mountaineers. It no longer takes
guests, but climbers can stay at the BMC
Memorial Hut nearby or at the camp-site near
Loch Brittle.

Loch Brittle

A clearly marked track leads from the
neighbourhood of Glen Brittle House to this
lonely sea-loch to the west of the southern
Coolins. It makes a good easy walk after
strenuous days in the hills.

The island
of Rhum
(overleaf)

From the cliffs beyond Glen Brittle the seaward
panorama is always rewarding, with the island
of Rhum, its main southern peaks clearly visible,
floating serenely on the rippling ocean.

Ruined church

Situated near Torrin on the road leading to
Elgol, this ruined church and old graveyard
nestle below the Beinn Deargs.

The view from Ord Bay

Moving north-east along the Sleat coast, the
superbly dark and jagged skyline of Blaven is
closer at hand than in the previous picture, and
even more impressive. Sgurr nan Gillean is
visible on the left.

Winter scene
(overleaf)

A bright cold day with snow on the tops and sunlight in the foreground, makes the most of the lovely lines of Blaven (spelled Bla Bheinn on some maps). The photograph was taken near Torrin.

Blaven and Clach Glas
(overleaf pp 132/133)

The splendour and wildness of Blaven's 3,000-ft summit, and the shattered crest of Clach Glas to the right, can fully be appreciated from the shores of Loch Slapin. The traverse of Blaven and Clach Glas is best undertaken from the Strathaird district across the loch.

The Coolins from Tarskavaig
(overleaf pp 134/135)

The same viewpoint as the picture on pages 126/127 provides this splendid view of the Black Coolins and their magnificent ridge – from Ghars-bheinn in the south to Sgurr nan Gillean in the north. The soft, opalescent atmosphere round the peaks is part of the characteristic charm of Skye.

Winter scene

(overleaf)

A bright cold day with snow on the tops and sunlight in the foreground, makes the most of the lovely lines of Blaven (spelled Bla Bheinn on some maps). The photograph was taken near Torrin.

Blaven and Clach Glas

(overleaf pp 132/133)

The splendour and wildness of Blaven's 3,000-ft summit, and the shattered crest of Clach Glas to the right, can fully be appreciated from the shores of Loch Slapin. The traverse of Blaven and Clach Glas is best undertaken from the Strathaird district across the loch.

The Coolins from Tarskavaig

(overleaf pp 134/135)

The same viewpoint as the picture on pages 126/127 provides this splendid view of the Black Coolins and their magnificent ridge – from Ghars-bheinn in the south to Sgurr nan Gillean in the north. The soft, opalescent atmosphere round the peaks is part of the characteristic charm of Skye.

Elgol

This remote hamlet on Strathaird, by the waters
of Loch Scavaig, provides (as we shall see on
the following pages) some of the most glorious
views of the Coolins range. Rearing up in the
background of the picture is Blaven.

Erosion at Elgol

This strange, almost honeycomb-like pattern has
been worn in the cliff by the action of the sea
over many thousands of years.

Cloud on the Coolins

(overleaf)

The main ridge of the Coolins begins in the south with the beautiful cone of Ghars-bheinn frowning down on Loch Scavaig. The great mass of shadowed and gleaming cumulus makes a wonderful background for this picture taken from Elgol.

Sun and snow

(overleaf pp 142/143)

The subtle shifts in the weather on Skye – the pageantry of rain, mist and sun – are part of the island's magic. In contrast to the previous picture, sunlight here reveals every detail of the Coolins and their splendid elevation on the edge of the restless sea.

Ghars-bheinn from the lake shore

(overleaf pp 144/145)

Movement in the foreground, and a figure to give a sense of scale to the majesty of the mountains beyond, all go towards making a memorable picture.

The Camasunary path starts here

From Camasunary on Loch Scavaig the
energetic walker can cross, via Glen Sligachan
which penetrates deep into the mountain
fastnesses, right through to Sligachan on the
eastern side of Skye, with scenes of grandeur all
the way.

Sgurr nan Gillean

On the Camasunary path there is a glimpse of
the head of Loch Scavaig, with darkening cloud
behind the Coolins and Sgurr nan Gillean.

Mountain mystery

(overleaf)

The secret beauty of the Coolins, born of their atmosphere and lighting, endears them to all mountaineers – but this is the only occasion on which I have seen such a cloud-formation here.

Sgurr nan Gillean from near Sligachan

(overleaf pp 152/153)

This picture was taken looking back at the twisting ridge and Sgurr nan Gillean near the end of the long walk from Camasunary. Where the snow has melted lower down the mountain flanks, it makes a fine colour contrast.

Mountain splendour

(overleaf pp 154/155)

This lochan near Sligachan is a favourite viewpoint of mine, and makes an excellent foreground for this picture of Sgurr nan Gillean lightly decked with snow.

View from Sligachan Bridge

From here Sgurr nan Gillean is seen at its best,
as a majestic cone of bare rock towering above
the intervening stretches of billowy moorland.
Its ascent by the favourite Tourist Route starts
near this bridge.

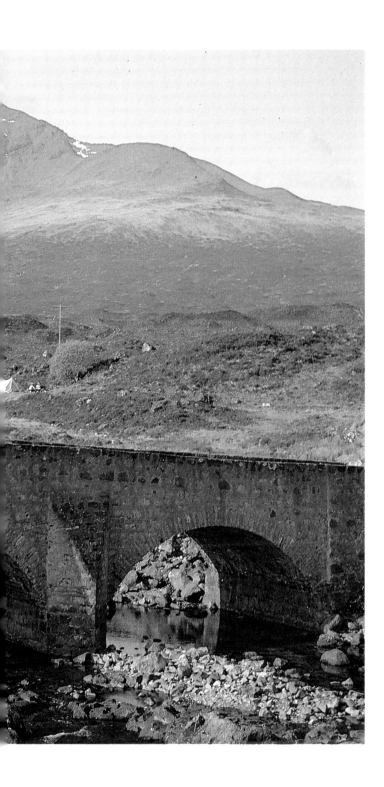

The Main Ridge

The precipitous, jagged and narrow Main Ridge
of the Coolins, snaking away from Sgurr nan
Gillean in the foreground, is famous throughout
the mountaineering world and calls for
experience, strength, and sureness of foot and
eye on the part of those who tackle it.

Knight's Peak

Seen in the centre of the photograph, and part
of the Pinnacle Ridge, this peak should not be
attempted by the unskilled climber. To the left
of the peak is Sgurr nan Gillean.

Pinnacle Ridge from the path to Bruach na Frithe

(overleaf)

The striking topography of Pinnacle Ridge is clearly seen in this photograph, with the peaks outlined against a cloudless sky.

Pinnacle Ridge from Sgurr a'Bhasteir

A fine picture of wild mountain grandeur taken
late on an autumn afternoon: the spectacular
structure of the Ridge is well seen from this airy
vantage point.

I reach
the summit

(overleaf)

The reward of a good hard day's climbing is the sensational vista that greets the mountaineer on arrival at the summit of Am Basteir. In front of me in this picture is the peak of Sgurr a'Bhasteir.

Am Basteir

This forbidding pyramid of rock, sometimes
known as 'the Executioner', rises from the
Coolins Main Ridge to the east of the Bealach
a'Bhasteir, and to the south of Sgurr nan Gillean
which is seen in this picture on the right.

The Basteir Tooth

This jagged pinnacle, adjacent to Am Basteir
itself, is of considerable fame in the
mountaineering world, not so much because of
its striking elevation as for the difficult course it
offers the rock climber.

The track to Bruach na Frithe

(overleaf)

Probably the only route to the Coolins Main
Ridge for non-climbers leaves the Sligachan-
Drynoch road and traverses somewhat boggy
moorland into Fionn Choire. From there a
cairned track leads easily to the summit of
Bruach na Frithe.

Bruach na Frithe from the Sgurr nan Gillean West Ridge

In the centre of this photograph, lying between Sgurr a'Fionn Choire to the north and Sgurr na Bairnich to the south, is the peak of Bruach na Frithe. From its summit cairn the climber will have one of the finest viewpoints in the Coolins, with a striking prospect of Blaven as well as of the great twists in the Main Ridge to the south.

Coire na Creiche

(overleaf)

The architecture of this barren wilderness of rock is on the grand scale, and it is near enough to Sligachan to be well worth a visit. The central peak, Sgurr an Fheadain, is split vertically by the famous Waterpipe Gully.

Coire na Banachdich

(overleaf pp 178/179)

This corrie may be easily explored from Glen Brittle. It is enclosed by Sgurr nan Gobhar, seen on the left, and by Sgurr Dearg on the right. The circuit of the corrie via these two peaks includes part of the Main Ridge of the Coolins.

Sgurr nan Gobhar Ridge

This offshoot of the Main Ridge can be reached
by walking over the moorland from Glen
Brittle: an exhilarating ascent of the ridge of
Sgurr nan Gobhar leads up to the summit of
Sgurr na Banachdich (right).

Sgurr nan Gobhar

The evening sunlight beautifully illuminates the
lower slopes of Sgurr nan Gobhar, seen here to
advantage in an 'end-on' view from the
moorland north of Glen Brittle.

The path to Coire Lagan

The walk to this wild corrie is one of the easiest from Glen Brittle, meandering over the moors and passing the lovely Eas Mor waterfall en route. Once at the corrie you are in the heart of the southern Coolins, with vast scree slopes fanning out into the corrie basin, as seen in the next picture.

Coire Lagan

This lonely corrie is surrounded by some of the grandest and most difficult peaks in the Coolins: Sgurr Alasdair, the highest mountain in the range, is on the right, Sgurr Thearlaich in the centre, and Sgurr Mich Coinnich on the left.

Looking along the Main Ridge

(overleaf)

Climbers who tackle the twisting Main Ridge of the Coolins from south to north can pause at this point, near their journey's end, and look ahead along the peaks to Sgurr nan Gillean in the distance.

Farewell

(overleaf pp 190/191)

The circular tour of this fascinating and magical island ends where it began, at the Kyle of Lochalsh, with a last look across the blue waters to the misty mountains of Skye.